IMPROVING SCHOOLS

7 Insider *Secrets*

TRANSFORM YOUR LOW-PERFORMING ELEMENTARY SCHOOL AND SCORE AN **A** IN RECORD TIME

Dr Janice Scott Cover

Copyright ©2013, Janice Scott Cover

All Rights Reserved. This book or any portion thereof may not be reproduced or used in any manner whatsoever without the express written permission of the author or publisher except for the use of brief quotations in a book review.

ISBN 978-976-95510-4-6

www.drjanicecoverbooks.com

First Printing, 2013

Published by: minna PRESS

Executive Editor: Lena Joy Rose

Copy Editor: Ayshah Johnston

Cover/Interior Design: Mark Steven Weinberger

Printed in the United States of America

Bulk Ordering: This book is available at special quantity discount to use for sales promotions, employee premiums or educational purposes. Contact: booksales@minnapress.com

DEDICATION

*To all educators around the world
who change lives every day.*

*To Baby Elise, for a bright, healthy, and productive future.
Dream big and work hard.*

It has been my philosophy of life that difficulties vanish when faced boldly. —*Isaac Asimov*

CONTENTS

About the author	viii
Preface	x
Introduction	15

FACE THE BRUTAL FACTS

Assess the situation	21
Apply standardized testing	22
How schools cope	23
Analyze the data	25
Point the blame	28

BEGIN AT THE BEGINNING

Get buy-in	31
Hire effective teachers	33
Know the curriculum	34
Develop clear measurable goals and objectives	35
Maximize time on task	38
Collaborate to motivate	38
Use schedules wisely	39
Engage non-instructional personnel	40
Set the tone	41
Establish unified discipline processes and procedures	41
Partner with parents	42
Organize tutorials	42
Align all budgets	43

CREATE A FOCUSED LEARNING ENVIRONMENT

Plan outcome based meetings	45
Graph students' progress	47
Organize relevant professional development	50
Partner with other schools	50
Configure chalkboard messages	50
Align school-age (after school) child care program	51
Use the public address system	52
Challenge the principal	53
Teach the discipline plan	53
Amplify academic support	54
Enrich and remediate using technology	55
Give homework	55
Monitor kindergarten through second grades	55

TEACH TEST TAKING SKILLS AND STRATEGIES

Activities before testing	59
Activities during testing	63
Activities for administrators	65

ANSWER THE QUESTION…ARE WE THERE YET?

Check individual student progress	69
Evaluate stakeholders' feedback	70
Identify remaining challenges	71
Stay on track with a checklist	71
Ask and answer the hard questions	72
Intensify monitoring and support	74

LEAD WITH A PURPOSE

Create a vision	77
Be courageous	77
Continuously learn	78
Reward achievements	79
Communicate effectively	79
Embrace diversity	80
Be accountable	80
Be resourceful	81
Be proactive	81
Epitomize integrity	84
Build trust	84

CELEBRATE TO STIMULATE

Motivate using accountability	87
Acknowledge individual and group achievement	88
Make rewards tangible	89
Accentuate academic achievements	90
Highlight performance and support employees	91
Lessons Learned	95
Conclusion	105
Bibliography	109
Recommended readings	110
Newspaper and other headlines	112
Acknowledgements	113

ABOUT THE AUTHOR

Dr Janice Scott Cover has spent most of her professional life working in urban school systems. Her life's calling has been to provide and support the means through which all students can achieve high standards. Named one of South Florida's Most Influential & Prominent Women, she has been featured in the Principal Magazine as a "Turn-Around Principal."

Currently, Dr Cover is the President & CEO of Improving Schools Consulting Services whose mission is to partner with schools to significantly improve student achievement. Previously, she has served as a teacher (K-12), assistant principal, principal, director of elementary education, assistant superintendent, area superintendent and district equity coordinator.

Her work includes developing and implementing a reform model that dramatically turned around an elementary school, resulting in significant academic and behavioral improvements, as well as fostering positive changes in teacher performance. She was actively involved in the design and opening of the first career alternative education school in the district. She also has expertise in designing and implementing unique after-school, Saturday and summer school enrichment and remediation programs.

A graduate of Moneague Teacher's College (Jamaica), she received a B.S. in Elementary Education from Louisiana State University. She earned a graduate degree in Educational Leadership, and also her Doctorate in Education with concentration in Child and Youth Studies from Nova Southeastern University. She has been a participant at the Harvard Institute for School Leadership and twice at the Darden/Curry School Executive Leadership Academy.

Dr Cover has presented at national and international conferences. She is the recipient of several awards: Lifetime Achiever in Education, Woman of Excellence and Lumina - Most Accomplished Community Leader as well as various entrepreneur awards.

A passionate philanthropist, Dr Cover founded the Caribbean Educators' Association whose mission is to make a positive difference in the lives of others through a supportive network of educators and other professionals. Through this organization, scholarships are awarded to qualifying high school graduates.

Dr Cover lives with her family in South Florida.

For more information:
  drcover@improvingschoolsinfo.com
  www.improvingschoolsinfo.com
  www.drjanicecoverbooks.com.

PREFACE

I strongly believe that I was born to teach. As a five year old child in rural Jamaica, I remember using the side of our house as a chalkboard and the students were the shrubbery, flowers and small plants that grew alongside the house. On the weekends and for many summers that was my classroom. I had a teacher voice and a student voice; asking and answering the questions myself. All my students were successful because I inherently believed it was my responsibility to make that happen.

During recess at my elementary school, I recruited my peers to be my students and I 'kept school.' I had a specific location where we would meet and I would rush to the spot each day to make sure the area was ready for school. My approach to teaching was more sophisticated than speaking to plants. Now my students were real and I had a curriculum; the one that my teacher used in our one room school house. Since we were in a one room school the classrooms were open and I had opportunities to observe the teaching styles of several teachers around me.

I absorbed classroom management skills, how to build rapport with students, how to differentiate instruction and just as important, the tone a teacher should use. I was an avid reader and very curious about the trade books being read in other classes; not only did I read many of their books but I became reading buddies with several of the teachers. In addition to being taken to exotic far- away places, this experience provided many positive role models and taught me that teachers are real people who must find ways to connect with their students.

My high school teachers recognized my gift for teaching and arranged for me to be a teacher/ helper at a neighborhood basic school when my school day was over. This experience heightened my awareness that teachers do much more than teach reading, writing, and arithmetic. These early experiences confirmed that my life's calling would be to teach.

As a trained classroom teacher in urban and rural areas within and outside of the United States, I used a variety of techniques to motivate and inspire my students to learn. I used real world experiences, provided my students with opportunities to dialogue with each other, took them on nature walks and field trips to explore their environments, asked them thought provoking questions and got them to write continuously. They read with me, with each other and independently. We read a lot. We had review sessions before each test and I held myself accountable for their progress. I taught in-depth subject content with the associated skills. I engaged students in debates, role playing and current events. My students became experts at cooperative learning.

In my own way, I helped students believe in their own abilities as I demonstrated that I believed in them. I communicated regularly and openly with parents. I had ongoing discussions with my peers to get strategies to improve my skills. Over time I developed the reputation of being a master teacher. Parents overwhelmingly made requests for their children to be in my classes and my peers and supervisors saw me as a star teacher.

With my transition to school level administration I carried my core belief that I was vital to the success of my students. As a principal, I had a bigger platform and could positively impact more students on a daily basis. I operated from the premise that the school was my large classroom and I worked even more diligently to help students succeed by:

- Monitoring instruction and student progress.
- Using multiple data sources to make a variety of instructional and administrative decisions and holding everyone accountable for student achievement.
- Remaining resolute to the fact that all children will learn and achieve at high standards with the appropriate instruction in a favorable learning environment.

My successes as teacher and principal provided a solid foundation and created the opportunity to apply my skills in the elementary school system which is the major focus of this book.

I wrote the book for two specific audiences:

- **Educators**—providing them with proven and practical strategies that will significantly improve student achievement and improve school ratings.
- **Policy makers, education advocates, government and other institutions** who make a difference in the lives of children. They will understand that schools serving a significant number of children who live in poverty need consistent, adequate and sustainable funding along with curriculum and instructional practices that meet their countless academic and social needs.

A teacher is the most important factor in student achievement. For this reason, the teaching staff of the featured elementary school in the book was restructured and only teachers who demonstrated that they could significantly improve student achievement with similar student populations were hired. It is imperative that teacher instructional practices align with the needs of students they teach. As Jim Collins (2001) told us in his book, *Good to Great,* leaders should 'Get the right people on the bus'.

I got the 'right people on the bus' and together we created a school culture that had high expectations, was accountable and supportive, and we accepted no excuses. This recipe resulted in the dramatic improvement of student academic and behavior performances and our school achieving its first A rating.

INTRODUCTION

Many urban elementary schools are in crisis. School administrators are constantly challenged to meet the ever changing local, state and federal educational requirements. Urban schools tend to have revolving doors for administrators, teachers and students. It appears that educators who work in urban settings are always fighting an uphill battle in the teaching and learning process.

Background of failing schools

Many children in urban school settings live in poverty and often come to school with limited school readiness skills. They are more likely from environments that lack resources to help them develop as healthy persons. Their parents or guardians often find themselves in a struggle to survive and to provide the basic needs of food, shelter and clothing. As a result, education is pushed further down on their list of priorities and the burden falls on schools to teach not only the academic skills but assist in the development of other attributes that will facilitate the children's overall growth and success.

An elementary school in crisis

This book will take you on the journey of an urban elementary school with a very diverse student population.

However, it is plagued with underachievement, frustrated educators, and a fairly disengaged community. The school district was willing to support an approach that would drastically change the downward spiral, and a principal who has embraced the belief that failure for any child is never an option.

A Memorandum of Understanding (MOU) between the school board and the classroom teachers' association cleared the way for the implementation of a four year pilot program based on a reform model geared toward dramatically improving student achievement. Under the reform model the school would be reconstituted; changing the majority of the teaching staff; aligning resources that were already at the school to pay teachers more for working an additional 175 hours that included tutoring students, participating in collaborative planning, professional development, parent meetings and conducting home visits. Importantly, there would be a strategic and systematic focus on the curriculum; particularly in the areas of reading, writing, and mathematics. The book highlights the school-wide strategies, processes and procedures employed in the successful turnaround of the elementary school.

**So what is the story of the school?
Why was it necessary to make this drastic change?**

School characteristics

"X" Elementary School is a public, urban school located in southeastern USA and was built in 1966. This neighborhood school serves kindergarten through fifth grade children who walk, ride their bikes, or are transported by parents or community child care agencies. The following data shows the school

Year	White	Black	Hispanic	Free/ Reduced	Limited English Proficient (LEP)	Exceptional Student Education (ESE)	Absent Rate
1999	15	69	13	80	37	9	5
2000	17	66	13	81	37	9	5
2001	13	69	14	82	40	9	4
2002	10	73	13	83	45	10	5
2003	3	80	13	92	46	12	3

Data above shows a decline in enrollment of Caucasian students, an increase of Black students, and no significant changes in the number of Hispanic students. The poverty rate has increased. The absentee rate fluctuated. Both the LEP and ESE populations are steadily rising.

demographics for five years leading up to the implementation of the Reform Model.

Why change?

In the 1998-1999 school year the school became a Fine Arts Magnet School, receiving funding from the Federal Government to provide:
- A unique learning opportunity for students
- To integrate the student population, and
- To improve student achievement

In addition to the requirements of the core curriculum subjects of language arts (reading, writing, listening, speaking and viewing), mathematics, science and social studies, all students were required to participate in approximately one and a half hours of performing and visual arts or arts related activity on a daily basis.

Year	School Grade
1999	D
2000	D
2001	D
2002	C

For three years starting in 1999 the school grades and student scores remained static but trending downward. In 2002 the overall points inched upward from a rating of 'D' (320 points) to 'C' 326 points.

For four years the school struggled to meet the state and district reading, writing and mathematics goals as well as those goals proposed in the federal grant.

The chart above gives an overview of the school's grades over a four year period.

The school also faced other challenges, for example, Caucasian students who were recruited for the arts programs left in droves after the first year of the implementation of the magnet program. There was also high turn-over of the instructional and administrative staff. Between 1998 and 2002 there was an average of 20 new teachers who transitioned each year. During the same time period there were approximately three assistant principal changes and just as frightening, within an eleven month period of time there were three principal changes. Each year it was like starting school all over rather than improving on strategies, procedures and processes that were already in place.

With the backdrop of low student achievement, high teacher and staff turn-over and declining student enrollment, change was needed. Hence, the development and implementation of the reform model that turned the school around.

The Reform Model

In 2002 the school was reconstituted by making significant changes to the instructional staff. Of the 57 teachers on staff, 37 were transferred to other schools within the district and the remaining twenty were joined by 37 new and experienced teachers who were selected through a rigorous interview process. The school's budget of $723,300 came from three sources: (i) the Federal Grant, (ii) the State, and (iii) the school district. These funds were used to pay a stipend to teachers, to expand professional development activities, to purchase needed materials and supplies and for any other school related expenses. The teachers were paid an additional stipend of $7,000 per year for four years. For this extra pay teachers had to commit to:

- Signing an agreement to remain at the school for four years, but could opt out after the first year.
- Working an additional 175 hours that would involve conducting home visits.
- Tutoring students beyond the regular work hours.
- Participating in professional development, and
- Holding parent meetings.

COMPONENTS OF THE REFORM MODEL

- Change school from an Arts Magnet School to Arts Theme School
- Reconstitute the instructional staff
- 175 hours completing extra duty responsibilities
- Reallocate the school's budget
- Implement a targeted curriculum
- Continuously monitor and assess instruction, student progress and classroom behavior.

The purpose of this book

This book was written to share an example of how a school can be successfully turned around when there is collaboration between school district, teachers' union, school center and school community. This book also serves as an appeal for the allocation of adequate funding and ample resources for urban schools and to create a sense of urgency around surrounding students with teachers who possess effective methodologies to meet the varying needs of their urban students.

The chapters in the book are designed so that you may go directly to a chapter for specific strategies or you may read the entire book to understand the comprehensive approach used in this simple school reform model. You will experience how data was used to identify needs, make changes in instruction, school operations, personnel and budgetary allocations. The book details the reform model's comprehensive, deliberate and purposeful laser-like approach. It shows the importance of teaching test taking skills and strategies; the enormous impact of effective leadership as well as how to celebrate large or small accomplishments and successes.

So whether you are looking for strategies to improve an entire elementary, middle or high school, grade levels within a school, individual classes or sub-groups of students, this book will provide proven and practical strategies to meet your school's needs. Let us get to the first chapter where the major transformation begins.

FACE THE BRUTAL FACTS

Assess the situation

Assessing student progress has been a natural part of the school experience since the nineteenth century. From those early years, teachers tested students to gauge mastery of the skills taught. For the most part, teachers wrote the test items or used end of chapter book tests. The results were primarily used to determine promotion from one grade to another or for retention in the same grade.

Teachers also used the sizing up method to get information about students. Sizing up is an informal and subjective observation process that is used by educators to gather information about students' academic and behavior performances. School boards very rarely got involved with test results. Teachers kept their own records so they would be able to prove that they taught and if the students were not successful they had only themselves to blame.

Over the years, there have been drastic changes in the reasons for and use of assessments. Today, assessments have several purposes that include providing feedback to students and families, informing instruction, developing curriculum and to maintain student records. Assessment results are also used by governing boards and policy makers to share pertinent information to their respective constituents.

The Elementary and Secondary Education Act of 1965 and the *No Child Left Behind Act* of 2001 mandated that standardized tests be administered in order for public schools to receive federal funding. Hence, standardized tests have become the norm in education systems in the United States. This has resulted in the curriculum and instruction for elementary and secondary schools being dominated by what children should know and be able to do to be successful in the test.

Apply standardized testing

This emphasis on standardized testing has created increased anxiety in education. Teachers have expressed disconnects between their practice and the requirements for the standards based test and many feel ill-prepared to meet the continuously changing testing requirements.

Many feel that the mandated focus on the test has robbed them of their creativity to teach. As for students, they are expected to meet preset grade level proficiency standards. There are exceptions for some students with special needs. Test results are also used for mandatory retention at specific grade levels as well as for graduation from high school. In several states and the State of Florida, test results are used to compare schools, often creating a sense of competition within and among schools.

Standardized test results have exposed academic achievement gaps which are used to fuel on-going education debates. Many states have performance grades for their schools and these grades are available to the viewing public who often make their own analysis and determine "good" and "bad" schools. With much debate swirling about the conundrum of public education, many parents express concerns about finding the "best" schools to send their children. The growing number of charter schools, school voucher programs, virtual education and increasing interests in home education, school choice has become a trend in education.

The relentless focus on standardized testing also takes its toll on schools and school districts. Frustrated with the growing challenges associated with assessment, teachers and administrators are sometimes reluctant to work in schools with high numbers of students whose test performance is less than desirable. Added to this is the yearly struggle, to understand and prepare students for the test that has constantly changing requirements and criteria.

National debates on public education that are centered on test scores show concerns about the performance of America's students compared to their counterparts in countries like China, India, Finland, Japan and Canada, to name just a few. Quite often these debates end with an outcry for public school reform.

How schools cope

It does not matter where your opinion rests on the standardized testing debate. It is obvious that assessment data is being used by schools in a variety of ways; some quite drastic and others more subtle to impact school improvement. Some focus their attention on school-wide interventions; some look at subgroups within the school's population while other schools target individual students. Here are some of the tactics that educators use:

⯈ Sophisticated data systems are developed to track

student, teacher, and school district performances.

❥ Varied professional development activities for school personnel are now part of school cultures.

❥ School personnel are being trained to analyze and use data to inform and improve instruction.

❥ Administrators are continuously making revisions to school budgets to provide needed resources. Personnel decisions include assigning instructional staff based on needs of students.

❥ Strategic monitoring of classroom instruction and teacher evaluation are at the top of school administrators' daily tasks. Pressures and expectations are trickling down from state departments of education to school districts that pass them onto schools.

My conversations with educators about how they are doing, usually lead to expressions of frustrations, undue stress and helplessness because they struggle to meet local, state and federal education requirements.

With the lagging student performance and other negative school factors, I was given the opportunity to develop a plan that would improve the school's state of affairs. I jumped at the opportunity to reform the school. With my "failure is not an option" attitude, I set out on a course of action to change the direction of our elementary school.

At the outset I knew that my decisions had to be based on assessment data. I also knew that I had to use my knowledge and skills in a systemic approach to change attitudes and beliefs of everyone associated with our school. I knew without a doubt that the data would help all the stakeholders arrive at the conclusion that a drastic change was needed.

Analyze the data

The first task tackled was to develop a working knowledge and understanding of the data. Experts from the district's testing and evaluation department provided a series of workshops. Note that I said a series, not a one shot occasion. We examined the data in many different ways

```
          Compare
            and
          Contrast
      ─────────────────
      Analyze Performance
    ─────────────────────────
   Assess Strengths and Weaknesses
```

Strengths and weaknesses in core tested subjects—reading, writing, and mathematics—were intensely analyzed. Not only did we analyze the performance of all student demographic subgroups but we also looked at how individual students across the accountability grades (three through five) were performing over time. Importantly, we studied and compared the results by classroom. This helped to show the impact of instruction and teacher style.

Simultaneously, we examined the performance of students in the primary grades (kindergarten to second grade). It was important for us to know students' performance levels as they progressed through to the intermediate grades. Teachers were taught how to find and analyze just in time data for the students currently in their classroom as well as for students who come in throughout the school term. Knowledge of individual student performance data is the place to begin the process of developing an individualized education action plan. Our school had a very migratory student population so keeping track of each student's academic performance was critical.

We compared our test scores to those of similar schools within the district and the state. We compared the proficiencies of each subgroup. Then we looked at the strategies outlined in the various schools' School Improvement Plans (SIP) and compared them to the strategies being included in our plan. Of course, our target was to be an "A" school so we also examined the strategies being used by schools that consistently achieved "A" ratings.

Our next task was to focus on the expectations of the test. Fortunately, we had access to the Florida State Department of Education's Item Specifications which is a road map to the Florida Comprehensive Assessment Test (FCAT). These subject specific documents outlined the content and format of the state assessment and showed the alignment to the Sunshine State Standards. Teachers participated in several subject and grade specific Item Specification professional development activities in order to get a deeper understanding of the test's criteria and requirements.

The writing rubric was also studied. Although writing was only tested in the fourth grade, the rubric was used by all second through fifth grade teachers in the school-wide writing plan. The writing plan focused on the writing process as well as vocabulary development.

SIX-POINT WRITING RUBRIC

6
- Fully addresses topic
- Stays on topic
- Utilizes specific examples with descriptive details
- Makes effective transitions that lead to a point
- Employs sentences of different lengths
- Makes few mistakes in grammar and spelling
- Utilizes vocabulary words effectively

5
- Fully addresses topic
- Stays on topic
- Utilizes specific examples with descriptive details
- Makes effective transitions that lead to a point
- Employs sentences of different lengths
- Makes few mistakes in grammar and spelling
- Utilizes vocabulary words effectively

4
- Introduction, body and conclusion mostly stay on topic, but may have one or two off topic ideas
- Utilizes some paragraphs
- Makes some transitions
- Details and points are evident, but not thoroughly explained
- Uses limited examples
- Makes few mistakes in grammar and spelling
- Utilizes vocabulary words effectively

3
- The introduction, body and conclusion are on topic
- Details are briefly explained
- Some points may be explained more thoroughly than others
- Some paragraphs evident
- Makes few mistakes in grammar and spelling
- Utilizes most vocabulary words effectively

2
- Stays somewhat on topic
- Introduction, body and conclusion are brief
- Details are sketchy
- Common words are usually spelled correctly but there may be grammar mistakes

1
- Wonders off topic/not really answering question
- Essay may not seem complete; leaves the reader hanging
- Supporting ideas are expressed in general terms and not fully developed
- No real details evident
- Common words used incorrectly
- Numerous errors in grammar and spelling

0
- Barely on topic or not at all
- Handwriting not legible
- Written in a foreign language
- Essay does not make sense

Adapted from the Florida Department of Education website

After the development of a working knowledge and understanding of the state test and how to access the data, our attention was turned to facing the brutal facts about the performance of our students; where they are and where they should be, not just for individual progress and promotion, but with improving the overall school performance and grade. This process created some levels of discomfort.

Point the blame

Before the restructuring of the teaching staff, a variety of reasons were given for why students were underperforming.

» Some teachers thought parents needed to be more involved in their children's education like coming to school and helping with homework.

» Other reasons included blaming previous teachers for not adequately preparing the students.

» Teachers also blamed their peers for coming to work late and leaving early – not being loyal to the school and students; they criticized each other for not being actively engaged in school activities.

» School discipline was also on the list of complaints. Some teachers accused their peers of being afraid of the students, hence, the breakdown in discipline.

» Lack of empathy for people living in poverty was also a point of discussion.

» School administration was not exempted from the blame game. The administration was accused of not sending home the "bad" children; for being too soft on

DATA SOURCES

State	Standardized tests
District	Kindergarten to Third Grade assessments
	Running records
	Computer generated reading and mathematics reports
	Common assessments
School	Teacher developed weekly assessments

discipline; for handing down the many demands from the central office and for not being empathetic to teachers' plight of dealing with daily classroom stress.

We used a variety of data sources to diagnose and remediate. The data was instrumental in creating a sense of urgency for school reform. The data was also used as a tool to motivate. Since we were open to face the truths using the data, it was therefore unproblematic to develop and administer weekly assessments that were based on the standards and benchmarks of the weekly instruction. Importantly, the data made it apparent for the school to get additional support and resources from the school district. Without a doubt, the data was of tremendous benefit in helping to set the stage for the beginning of the school's transformation.

The data that drove the transformation came from a variety of sources as shown in the chart above.

YOUR ACTION PLAN AND CHECKLIST

Learn how to access student data

Identify all data sources

Analyze all available data

Identify strengths and weaknesses in the curriculum

Examine impact of individual classroom instruction

Examine performance of students in the intermediate grades

Examine performance of students in the primary grades

Compare scores with other similar schools within district and state

Research school improvement strategies of other schools

Study and learn the expectations in each subject area of the state test

Organize data centered professional development activities

BEGIN AT THE BEGINNING

I associate the processes of a drastic school turnaround with that of preparing for and running the first marathon. In both situations, the first task is to assemble a team of experts and bring together a support system. Next, develop a plan with clear measurable and attainable goals. Finally, engage in a course of ongoing practice and reevaluation of performance and finally, methodically execute the plan.

The first chapter focused on the driving force behind school improvement, the school's data. Before a school embarks on a reform process, it is important to know what the current data shows versus what it should be. This chapter will outline strategies on how to get organized in preparation for the huge yet exciting task of turning around the school.

Get buy-in

An African proverb reminds us that, "it takes a village to raise a child." Well, it also takes a village to turn around a school. Getting buy-in from all stakeholders (child, instructional and non-instructional staff members, parents, community, and school district) is critical. There are several ways to achieve this shared responsibility. At the beginning of our school's turnaround process, one of the first steps that we took was to hold separate meetings tailored to the various stakeholder groups.

At the meetings we shared the reform model, along with the dismal data which ignited its development; got feedback and asked for support. There was a recorder and language translator present at each meeting. Having a translator was important because almost half of the students were English Language Learners (ELL). Each meeting ended with a review of the main discussion points. Additionally, we set follow-up meeting dates and distributed contact information for school personnel so meeting participants could communicate with any additional questions or suggestions.

We set up group and individual meetings with third through fifth grade students so they could get information on their academic and behavior performance over time. Because of privacy policies only general school-wide information was shared in the whole group sessions. Each student participated in individual sessions with particular teachers. I was present at the meetings as much as my schedule allowed. The guidance counselor participated for targeted students. All students were given the opportunity to share their thoughts about their achievements, after which, academic and behavioral goals were established and, in some cases, contracts were developed and signed with identified students.

At the same meeting, students were asked to respond to a two-item survey. The first question asked was, "If you had three wishes what would they be? List them in priority order."

The second was, "If you got ten dollars, how would you spend it?" The results of the survey were used in the students' incentive plan which will be discussed later.

FIVE CHARACTERISTICS OF AN EFFECTIVE TEACHER

1. Positive expectations
2. Enthusiasm
3. Effective classroom manager/organization
4. Ability to design lessons and activities
5. Rapport with students

Hire effective teachers

The most important school variable to student achievement is the effectiveness of the teacher.

It is therefore incumbent on school administrators to place students in classrooms where they will get the most appropriate instruction to meet their learning needs. This means it may be necessary to make changes in some teacher assignments. Like other decisions in the turnaround process, data should be used in the placement of students and the reassignment of teachers. As a former school building administrator I know that personnel issues like the reassignment of teachers is an enormous leadership challenge. In some school systems school administrators have the authority to assign teachers at will, while in other systems they may have to work with the teachers' union, and/or the union building representatives to change teacher assignments.

In our reform model, we included the teachers' union and the school district labor relations personnel at the onset of our planning. My advice is to review the teacher contract before attempting to reassign teachers or embarking on any school-wide changes. From personal experience I know that taking on this challenge will not be pleasant but it is critical to the success of students.

After the instructional staff is in place, teacher leaders and the specific academic teams identified, team building exercises should begin. All school personnel should be involved in the team building activities. It will be worthwhile to get the services of an expert to help build camaraderie between and among the various school groups. The newly formed teams should analyze the data for their respective grade levels, for individual classrooms within the grade and for individual students. School district's privacy policies should be reviewed before sharing student information.

Know the curriculum

With teachers in place and equipped with a working knowledge of students' performance and ability levels, it is time to focus on the curriculum standards. Understanding the standards and the related benchmarks for each grade level is essential in the organization and preparation process. This will help everyone know what students should know and be able to do, not just for the test but for successful progression through school. The Sunshine State Standards (SSS) were our guide, as were the Florida Comprehensive Assessment Test (FCAT) Item Specifications documents that detail the format and content as well as assessment items for specific subjects and grade levels. All state departments of education provide information on the state standardized test. So in the absence of a document like the Item Specification, a detailed review of the standards should provide valuable curricula information.

Armed with the curriculum standards, Item Specifications or similar document and a blank calendar, you are now ready to develop a scope and sequence plan correlated with a school calendar. The development of this scope and sequence will be advantageous to both experienced and new teachers as they develop a map outlining what should be taught and when. This will also be helpful to school administrators in the monitoring of classroom instruction. Another advantage of a scope and sequence is to guide the development of the weekly assessments. Weekly assessments will be discussed in more detail in the third chapter.

In this organizational phase the curriculum benchmark data should be one tool used to group students for classroom instruction and tutorial support. Likewise, benchmark data also provides information on strengths and weaknesses in classroom instruction which will drive topics for professional development. Schools should look at multiple years' results of curriculum benchmark data across grade levels to identify areas of need.

In the planning of the curriculum and its implementation, particular attention must be paid to the physical layout of classrooms. Students must have easy access to equipment and materials. Grouping for instruction may also require modifications to the physical arrangement of classrooms.

Develop clear measurable goals and objectives

The objectives that drove our school improvement plan defined our course of action, helped us to stay true to the mission and provided an objective tool when adjustments were necessary. The school's data showed where improvements and interventions were needed and the state standards provided the expectations. With this information, we were able to design clear, specific and measurable goals and objectives. The Specific, Measurable, Achievable, Realistic and Time-bound (S.M.A.R.T.) format was used to guide the development of the objectives.

A sample writing objective looked like this:

By the end of February at least 90% of fourth grade students will meet or exceed the writing standard of 3.0 as evidenced by the FCAT.

This objective was **Specific** to the targets (writing and fourth grade students), it quantified a **Measurement** (90%), the trend data proved that it was **Achievable** and **Realistic** and the **Timely** goal was to meet or exceed the 3.0 standard for the test that was to be administered in February.

All fourth grade students knew the objective. Each student had a copy of the writing rubric affixed to his or her desk. Examples of high quality writings were read, discussed and used as models when students revised and edited their numerous practice essays. This writing process was done individually, with a buddy, in a cooperative group or with the entire class.

Similar objectives were created for reading and mathematics. Discussions at the planning and collaboration meetings included the progress that was being made toward the established objectives. The objectives were well known and to a great extent contributed to the solidarity and unification we experienced along our turnaround journey.

S.M.A.R.T. GOALS/OBJECTIVES

Specific
Write down your specific goal/objective. What is it you want to achieve? Even though the ultimate goal is to score an "A" rating, establish smaller goals and objectives along the way to drive momentum.

Measurable
Evaluate and quantify the results of your goals and objectives along the way. Track the progress and measure the outcomes. What percentage needs improvement and what is succeeding? You should be able to answer the questions—how many? How much?

Attainable
Goals and objectives should be attainable and assignable. Are all the resources in place or can be put in place to make the goal achievable? Who will be assigned (individuals or teams) to implement this goal?

Realistic
Based on your available resources and data, is this goal feasible? Examine your data and determine ways to improve your chance of success.

Time-bound
Not only set the ultimate deadline for scoring the "A" rating but also set minor deadlines along the way, for example:
- Needs assessment completed by October 15
- Establish goals and objectives by November 30
- Get buy-in from stakeholders by January 31.

Continue setting these deadlines until the big goal is achieved.

Maximize time on task

Time on task is vital to teaching and learning, so attention must be paid to the efficient use of time. Every minute of the school day is valuable to the teaching and learning process. All schedules must therefore be examined and revised, prioritizing the use of instructional time. Allocating sufficient instructional time and time for student engagement during instruction are paramount to student success. Teachers should be given adequate uninterrupted time for teaching, re-teaching and providing feedback. Instructional time should be considered sacred and this should be communicated to everyone. For example:

> ⟩ During instruction, there should be no general announcements on the public address system except in cases of emergencies.
>
> ⟩ There should be no unnecessary interruptions in the form of visits to classrooms.
>
> ⟩ Mundane tasks like taking attendance and making lunch choices should be done either first thing in the morning or through a check off system done by individual students as they enter their classrooms. An activity as simple as collecting homework should be done in a manner that will not consume valuable instructional time. The more organized a teacher, the more efficient she will be with the use of time.

Collaborate to motivate

After our successful turnaround, an external evaluation was conducted on the reform model used. Overwhelmingly,

teachers had positive comments about the impact of common planning and collaboration that took place with school staff including school administrators. This helped to reaffirm the importance of communication within and across grade levels. To make the meetings purposeful, they should be:
- Planned collaboratively.
- Structured with agendas, specific goals, objectives and expected outcomes.
- Staff attendance should be mandatory.
- Discussions at these meetings should be centered on student academic progress. and behaviors that are impacting learning.

One outcome of the collaboration meetings should be the identification of professional development topics.

Building trust is one of the great benefits of a collaborative school culture. For example, a meeting agenda item may focus on samples of students' work, assessment results, documentation of observable behaviors and any and all issues that impact student achievement. This dialogue may expose weaknesses in instruction and/or classroom management. Therefore, participants must feel safe in order for honest discourse and resolution to take place.

Use schedules wisely

Strategic scheduling of non-academic subjects like lunch and fine arts offers many benefits. These include maximizing time, providing opportunities to coordinate grade level academic activities and allowing for common planning and teacher collaboration. School schedules should also include time for before, during and after school academic support.

Engage non-instructional personnel

Every adult who interacts with the students must be included in the development and implementation of the processes and procedures as the school prepares for the reform. This includes non-instructional personnel.

At "X" Elementary School, non-instructional personnel also called members of the support staff, included paraprofessionals, cafeteria workers, bus drivers, custodians and clerical staff. We acknowledged that the value they bring to the growth and development of students is immeasurable and they played a variety of roles.

- Paraprofessionals were trained to help with academic enrichment and remediation.
- Cafeteria workers encouraged students to make healthy food choices and taught dining etiquette.
- Custodians provided a clean and aesthetically pleasing environment which undoubtedly contributed to student performance and behavior.
- The bus drivers' role was two-fold; taking students to school on time as well as providing a pleasant morning ride to start the school day on a positive note.
- Secretaries set the tone for a pleasant front office experience for students, parents and visitors.

In addition to their respective roles and positions, non-instructional staff members should be trained as mentors. They were important in our reorganization from the beginning; they welcomed the inclusion, embraced the responsibilities, took ownership and celebrated in the successes.

Set the tone

While everyone must be partners in the organization process, school administrators are the standard bearers. They set the tone, must be constant cheerleaders, trouble shooters and the consummate leaders of change. They too must be flexible and model positive change in their communication, behaviors and attitudes. All the school administrators and leaders must present a unified front. In our case, the assistant principal focused much of her time on the monitoring and evaluation of the primary grades while I, the principal, paid exceptional and unwavering attention to the students and teachers in the accountability grades three through five. We both met regularly. Because the role of the administrators is paramount to a successful school turnaround, an entire chapter in this book is dedicated to characteristics of effective leadership.

Establish unified discipline processes and procedures

It is no secret that learning will not take place in a chaotic, undisciplined, disorganized and disrespectful school environment. So a school-wide discipline plan with input from all stakeholders, including the students, should be developed, displayed, taught and constantly practiced. The concept of a school-wide discipline plan must be emphasized because there should be consistency in all classrooms, on the playground, in the cafeteria, in the hallways, on the school bus and during extracurricular activities. Parents should be asked to include items from the school's plan in their home routines. Affective training included cultural competence and how to build a unified school culture.

Partner with parents

Parents are equal partners in the education of children and should be treated as partners in the restructuring process. So, there should be effective, appropriate and on-going communication and collaboration with parents and guardians. Meetings should be held at different times to accommodate varying schedules. Also, different types of meetings should be held. For example, curriculum, instruction and assessment meetings should help parents understand criteria, expectations and the requirements for the state, district and school tests and should show how the students are being prepared. We scheduled midterm and end of term conferences not including regularly scheduled parent teachers meetings. Another way we communicated with parents was by using daily agenda books. Students recorded their homework, and teachers and parents used agenda books as another forum to communicate general information about children. Parents signed the books daily. This method of communication was so important that we bought a book for every student each year.

Organize tutorials

During this organization phase we also identified students who needed additional academic support. Students were organized for tiered support using their academic performance levels. Students showing the greatest needs got an early tutorial start and others were included in the tutorial sessions as the time got closer to the test. We used research based commercially produced printed educational materials that were not being used in the regular curriculum. We also used computer software. The primary tutors were teachers who were selected based on their performance data. They were also trained on how to use the supplemental materials. In the evaluation, teachers also had positive comments about the program's structure and materials used in the tutorial program.

Align all budgets

Another critical component in the organization phase is the development of a budget. In addition to the alignment of resources, a budget will help to show where needs exist and therefore help to garner additional resources. It will also allow for the early purchase of needed materials, equipment and services outlined in the reform plan.

In this chapter, the groundwork was laid to begin the school's transformation. With a task so immense, getting buy-in, which leads to unconditional engagement from all stakeholders, is essential. Creating a community of learners helps to build camaraderie, trust and a unified purpose. Serious school reform requires revolutionized thinking, attitudes and beliefs about teaching and learning. Setting the tone for this transformation requires making the necessary changes in school personnel, daily school operations, aligning resources to the goals and objects of the plan and valuing the contributions of all persons who interact with the students. Above all, diagnosing students' needs and developing a plan of action with measurable goals and objectives must be at the core of the plan and should drive all decisions.

YOUR ACTION PLAN AND CHECKLIST

Assemble the winning team

Diagnose student needs

Learn the curriculum expectations for each grade level

Establish S.M.A.R.T. goals and objectives

Develop curriculum scope and sequence

Communicate the plan to all stakeholders

Get buy-in from stakeholders

Conduct data chats with students

Get input from students on creating an incentive plan

Make necessary changes in school personnel

Organize team building activities

Make necessary changes in daily school operations

Align resources to the goals and objectives

Train stakeholders on school-wide discipline plan

Value contributions of stakeholders

Design and establish parent and community outreach programs

Organize for student tutorial sessions

CREATE A FOCUSED LEARNING ENVIRONMENT

All actions taken and decision made in a turn-around journey should be deliberate and purposeful but none should have a more strategic focus than those that directly impact teaching and learning.

In the previous chapter I discussed the structural requisites that should be in place in preparation for an effective and successful school reform. The concentration in this chapter will be on teaching the curriculum, monitoring instructional practices and the ongoing assessment of and for instruction. All the strategies in this chapter were used in our school's speedy and triumphant transformation.

Plan outcome based meetings

On-going strategic and collaborative planning meetings were held. Two types of grade level planning meetings were held each week. The first meeting held was to brainstorm instructional strategies that would be used to teach the identified benchmark skills for the week. The strategies had to include activities for enrichment, remediation, re-teaching and accommodations for students with special needs. While teachers had the option to add strategies of their own to meet the needs of the individual students within their respective classrooms, everyone had to use the agreed upon strategies from the brainstorming sessions.

Teachers were expected to be present and be prepared for all meetings. They had to bring an adequate number of photo copies of researched based activities to teach the skills that would be discussed. The physical education, music, visual arts, writing, science, mathematics and computer teachers also had to bring copies of strategies and activities they would use to reinforce the week's skills in their respective subject areas.

Using the required subject content and the benchmark skills to be taught that week, teachers also designed weekly assessments. At this same meeting, each teacher contributed items for the test and the team leaders created the test which was submitted to me for approval. The types and rigor of questions, length of reading passages, and vocabulary used had to follow the format outlined in the Item Specifications of the state standardized test. These grade level specific tests were administered to all students at the respective grade level. Based on special needs requirements, we made accommodations for qualifying students. All students were expected to score 85% or greater on each test which was usually administered on Thursday or Friday. Teachers had results ready by Monday morning in preparation for the next team meeting.

The focus of the second round of team meetings was to discuss the results of the test that was administered the previous week. An in-depth test item analysis was conducted. Whole classroom and individual performances were compared and strengths and weaknesses discussed. Teachers also shared the instructional strategies they believed had the greatest impact on student performance. Decisions for re-teaching were made and on occasions, teachers with high percentage passing rates re-taught the skills to the classes that did not meet the established criteria. Students also became teachers to help their peers strengthen skills.

Graph students' progress

Students were expected to score at least 85% on all weekly tests and the results graphed by students, with teacher supervision. The graph was a visual that showed progress toward the weekly academic goals. A very simple bar graph format was used to record the reading, mathematics and writing scores. The graphing exercises served many purposes. In addition to reinforcing math skills, the graphs were a source of motivation, and one of the tools used by the teacher during data chats with students. The graphs also helped teachers get a quick snap shot of students' weekly progress and how to focus the re-teaching strategies. Each week, teachers met with individual students who scored less than 85%. At this meeting, students had to write a note, expressing why they thought they did not meet the 85% expectation and steps they would take to improve in the upcoming week.

Both the progress chart and the students' notes were submitted. I then met with the students to review their progress and their plan of action. I also met with teachers to discuss the plan of action to address weaknesses revealed as shown on the graphs. Students who scored 85% or better got their names entered into a weekly drawing which was part of the incentive plan. This simple graphing activity was widely lauded as one of the great contributors to the student academic gains. Several schools in the district now use this graphing technique in their school improvement initiatives.

STUDENT

Name _____

READING

Scale		1	2	3	4	5	6	7	8	9	Retest
	100										
	95										
	90										
	85										
	80										
	75										
	70										
	65										
	60										
	55										
	50										
	45										
	40										
	35										
	30										
	25										
	20										
	15										
	10										
Skill(s)											

GRAPH

Grade _____ Teacher _____

MATHEMATICS

Scale		1	2	3	4	5	6	7	8	9	Retest
	100										
	95										
	90										
	85										
	80										
	75										
	70										
	65										
	60										
	55										
	50										
	45										
	40										
	35										
	30										
	25										
	20										
	15										
	10										
Skill(s)											

Organize relevant professional development

Teachers received ongoing in-service to improve their content knowledge as well as knowledge of the standards and benchmarks. Experts from the school district's central office and teachers and or school administrators conducted training activities. Trainings were mandatory and there were always classroom based follow-up activities. Examples of follow up activities included the observed teaching of the skills learned in the in-service and documented in lesson plans. All professional development activities were directly aligned to the reform model.

Partner with other schools

Another strategy that proved quite valuable was the professional relationship that was established between our fourth grade teachers and fourth grade teachers at a nearby elementary school that continuously scored high on the state's writing test. Our elementary school partners graded the students' practice writing prompts and provided feedback not only to the students but also to the teachers. This activity proved to be a great opportunity for teacher to teacher professional development.

Configure chalkboard messages

Teachers wrote daily goals and objectives on the chalk board and attention drawn to them throughout the lessons. In addition to guiding what would be the instructional focus of the day, the objectives and goals were used during the feedback and reflection session which took a variety of formats. Students used individual lap boards to share what they learned; or they responded to questions which were led either by their peers or the teacher. This was an exciting activity for many reasons; one being, it demonstrated the impact of students being active participants in their own learning and another, it served as a springboard for re-teaching or lesson review. As the year progressed, feedback and reflection sessions became automatic and very popular. Teachers became guides as students took the lead.

Each new day started with a review of the skills learned the previous day. I visited classrooms several times throughout the day to monitor instruction and student discipline. I made a point of leaving teachers a brief note about my observations or I invited them to meet with me at the end of the day for feedback.

Align school-age (after school) child care program

It did not take long before the entire school was transformed into a true learning community. One example was evident in the change taking place in the school age child care program:
> Before the transformation, the afterschool care program focused more on arts and crafts and recreation. Now, in addition to the fun activities, the after school care program implemented an aligned academic enrichment and remedial curriculum that was an expansion of the skills taught during the regular school day. Students got additional help in reading, writing and mathematics.

⇒ Another change was the way in which school parties were held. Classroom parties were still encouraged; however, they had to have an academic theme. For example, a math party would provide reinforcement in the skill areas of measurement, fraction, or percentages. Teachers and students would develop the academic activities for the class parties. At first there was some resistance but the idea got trendy very quickly.

⇒ It was also amazing to see teachers constantly researching and sharing best practices and when they discussed students, the language started to shift from focusing on what children could not do to what they were doing and doing well.

Use the public address system

The school operated a student-run television show that was broadcasted to the entire school each morning and on special occasions. As principal, I participated in this show every morning. I used this medium to set the tone for the day. I gave school updates, reminded the students of the day's academic and behavior expectations and thanked the staff for their hard work. I also wore a large visible sign of an "A" on my chest and on my back. This was a reminder to

the entire school that our goal was to be an "A" rated school and that all activities for the day should be geared toward meeting that goal.

The public address system was also used to reinforce academic skills. We presented math and vocabulary challenges and students had to share the answers with their teachers. It was not uncommon to hear students discuss the answers as they lined up for lunch or as they traveled to extracurricular activities. In addition to strengthening academic skills, the morning challenges drastically reduced the opportunities for off task behaviors while encouraging cooperative learning.

Challenge the principal

Another unifying force around the school was the challenge the students gave me. They dared me that if the school made an "A" grade I would run around the playfield three times and then kiss a pig that would be waiting for me at the finish line. Of course, they lived up to their end of the bargain, so I had no choice but do my sprint and kiss a huge pig while the entire school, members of the community and news media looked on.

Teach the discipline plan

In addition to teaching the curriculum content, the discipline plan was also taught and practiced. An amazing outcome of this was the more focused teachers got with academic expectations, the fewer discipline infractions occurred. It was one of the highlights of my career to see students doing self-talk or helping their peers to de-escalate and get back on track when incidents occurred. An external evaluation of the model showed that over seventy percent of teachers felt that student discipline improved dramatically as evident in the number and recurrences of inappropriate behaviors.

Amplify academic support

Intensive focus was placed on academic progress each week. When the data showed the need, extra time to reinforce academic skills was provided through tutorial sessions that were held before, during and after school. Some classroom teachers taught targeted students before the beginning of the school day. Many of these students either walked to school or were taken by their parents. Throughout the day paraprofessionals and volunteers, with teacher direction, served as tutors. Tutorial sessions were also held after school and on special Saturdays.

The Saturday sessions were a production onto themselves. The first group of students to be recruited for the Saturday morning sessions was those with the greatest academic needs. Primary teachers with a strong literacy background and positive reading results taught the students with the greatest reading needs.

This first group started in October, the second group joined them in December and the final group started in January after the holidays. The Saturday sessions were well attended, breakfast and snacks were provided by local businesses, and incentives were given. Parents participated as chaperones and volunteers. All teachers were involved in Saturday tutorials.

Enrich and remediate using technology

Students also got extra help by using computers which were either in classrooms or in the two labs. They also received additional academic support in the science and mathematics labs. These totally hands-on activities were all aligned to the skills being learned in the regular classrooms. The students practiced reading and writing skills in all subjects across the curriculum.

Give homework

Homework was assigned Monday through Thursday to give students another opportunity at practicing skills learned in class. We were cognizant that some students probably would not get help with their homework when they went home. To ensure that all students would be able to complete homework, teachers allowed 'homework help time' for students who needed the support.

Monitor kindergarten through second grades

While intense focus was on the teaching and learning in grades three through five, much attention was also given to the primary grades. A significant number of students came to school with limited reading readiness skills and many with English as their second language, so reading was a crucial curriculum target in the primary grades. A balanced approach to literacy was implemented. The literacy blocks emphasized reading, writing, speaking, listening and viewing with students actively engaged in their literacy development. Class size was reduced to a ratio of 15:1 during the literacy block. Schedules were designed so that instructional, staff who was not serving in the capacity of regular classroom teachers, would be available to teach during the literacy blocks. All teachers got extensive professional development in balanced literacy.

Primary grade students also became part of the support system for the students in the intermediate grades. The young children adopted a class in the upper grades. They consistently sent their adopted class positive drawings or notes of encouragement. The older students often practiced their reading and comprehension skills when they read to and discussed stories with the younger students.

The unyielding focus on student success transformed the school. It was noticeable that everyone worked toward the same goal with an unparalleled focus to help all students succeed. Teachers communicated with each other more than ever before. Students took pride in their work and behavior. The graphing of weekly test results with the expectations of attaining at least 85% kept them focused and motivated. Every moment of the

COMPONENTS OF BALANCED LITERACY

- Reading Aloud (Modeled Reading)
- Shared Reading
- Guided Reading
- Independent Reading
- Modeled or Interactive Writing
- Shared Writing
- Guided Writing (Writing Workshop)
- Independent Writing

school day was important and students were being given every opportunity to practice, enhance and remediate academic skills. Without a doubt, there was a bright spotlight shining on preparation for the state standardized test, but at the same time a very positive school climate emerged.

While it was extremely important to teach the content for all subjects and the skills necessary for success on the test, it was equally important to teach students the format of the test. Hence, test taking skills and strategies were taught in every subject. Chapter IV is dedicated to the teaching of test taking skills and strategies because of the significant impact on the boost in confidence this provided to our students.

YOUR ACTION PLAN AND CHECKLIST

Organize calendar to accommodate time for planning and collaboration

Establish expectations for meetings

Establish framework and expectations for weekly tests

Design and implement use of graph to document students' weekly performance

Train students on purpose and use of weekly graphs

Research nearby schools for collegial partnerships

Identify topics for ongoing professional development

Identify persons to conduct professional development

Establish framework for chalkboard configuration and classroom layout

Establish general guidelines for instructional practices (direct instruction, practice, feedback, review, re-teach, homework, etc.)

Arrange curriculum articulation meetings with regular and school-age child care teachers

Align computer assisted software to instruction

TEACH TEST TAKING SKILLS AND STRATEGIES

We focused intensely on the teaching and learning of targeted skills but we also needed to help students understand the format of the test in order to improve their confidence and reduce uncertainties. As a result, we also incorporated test taking tips and strategies in the daily classroom routines. All classes uniformly employed test taking skills and strategies in classroom instruction.

Sun-Sentinel, South Florida, February 21, 2001

Activities before testing

Students confront their fears of the state test.

Students were asked to write letters to their teachers or to the principal to express their fears about the test. They identified things like fear of failure which could lead to retention, disappointment in themselves if they did not meet proficiency, concerns for how their parents would respond if they failed, fear of being criticized by their peers, they were worried about letting their teachers down and were fearful that they would not remember the answers or forget what they learned. Staff met with individual students to help alleviate their fears. Without identifying the students some of the issues were discussed in whole group sessions so all students could benefit from the responses.

Students learn to judge time when responding to state test items. To address the issue of having adequate time to respond to test items, students participated in whole class timing experiments. Classroom timers were set for one, two or three minute intervals. After the timer was turned on students simply sat in silence and waited for the time to expire. They were then given generic practice test items to complete at one, two and three minute intervals. Students were given the opportunity to talk about how they used the time and what they learned about timing themselves during the test. This activity helped to lower the anxieties associated with how much time they had to answer a test item.

Practice makes perfect. The weekly tests, developed by the school, and the common assessments required by the school district were seen as practice for the state test. The test results were always analyzed and students were able to see their strengths and weaknesses. Teachers used the test results to re-teach as often as necessary. A variety of approaches were used to review the skills. For example, games were played, graphic organizers and mnemonic techniques were used, students developed practice tests items, and teachers used items from retired state tests, computer software provided individual practice and students had study buddies to help as needed.

Students were also taught to practice circling key words and highlighting important points. Outlining was another strategy learned when responding to essay type questions or for the writing test. Another practice tip especially for the reading test was to read the answers before reading the passage. This intense practice helped to build test endurance as well as confidence in students' test taking abilities.

Administer practice tests using a format similar to the state test. Most weekly tests and all school district required practice tests administered under conditions that were similar to those used during the state test. These procedures included timing, giving appropriate directions, providing accommodations and utilizing proctors. Students who required alternate testing locations were moved to the identified areas within the school. The early familiarization with test requirements, test proctors and room environment helped to lower the stress levels during the administration of standardized test.

Prepare parents for the test. Meetings should be held with parents to explain the expectations for the state test and how they can help at home. For example, the format of sample test items with correct answers should be shared with parents. Parents should be encouraged to read with and to their children. Parents should also be informed about the positive impacts of adequate rest, proper diet, and a peaceful home environment especially on test days. Just as important, parents should be encouraged to get the children to school on time especially during the days of the testing window. We had regularly scheduled curriculum meetings with parents and test preparation activities being implemented at the school were shared.

Teach relaxation techniques. On the morning of each test day, using the public address system, I shared meditating activities to help students relax. One of the students' favorite was for them to close their eyes and pretend to be in their favorite place. They would think about why this was their favorite place, how being in this place made them feel and to focus on each of the beautiful objects or scenery in this place.

Sun-Sentinel, August 17, 2003

Activities during testing

Create a school-wide testing environment. While students in the accountability grades were being saturated with tips and strategies for a successful testing experience students in the primary grades were also experiencing test-like conditions. They participated in quiet activities, sometimes taking teacher-made tests themselves. Movements in the hallways were expected to be mouse-like and testing signs were posted throughout the school. To show my commitment to this, I set up a temporary office in the hallway and completed my paperwork from that location. I switched hallways intermittently. My presence not only helped to maintain calm but sent a message that we were in this together.

Eat before the test. In addition to encouraging parents to provide a healthy breakfast, we worked with our school cafeteria to provide protein rich snacks which were given to all students before the test started. After which, students went on a bathroom break. The protein provided nutritional benefits to the brain but just as important the activity made students feel very special.

Read and follow directions carefully. Based on testing protocols, directions were read to students and they were also taught, and continuously reminded that they must listen carefully, read, and pay attention to all test directions.

Remain positive throughout the test. Students were encouraged to bring to school a tiny object that made them feel happy. The objects would be placed on the desk but could not be toyed with during the test. Some students brought their favorite pictures of themselves, of family members or pets. Some wore their favorite clothing. To help students calm themselves during periods of anxiety, breathing techniques were taught and practiced.

Use a process of elimination to answer multiple choice questions. Students were taught that whether they were responding to reading or mathematics test items they should read all the answer choices before choosing one. As well, in times of doubt, they should use the process of elimination to rule out the choices they believe are wrong. Along the same lines, students were taught that unless they have evidence that they made the wrong choice, the first time, they should stick with their first choice.

Skip questions that are difficult to answer at first read; go back to them later. Students were encouraged to answer the easiest questions first. Then return to the more difficult ones; making sure that in the end all questions have complete answers.

Not all students will finish testing at the same time. Students need to be aware that they will not all complete their test at the same time. Their goal should be to focus their attention on their test and not on their peers. For this reason, we expected students, who finish early, to review their answers, erase stray marks, put their heads on their desk, be sensitive to their peers who are still working and not to engage in distracting behaviors. Proctors monitored to ensure students were following the end of test rules.

Activities for administrators

In addition to the concentrated focus on teaching and practicing test taking tips and strategies, school administration took other actions to ensure a positive school testing environment. The principal completed the following tasks:

- Stopped all maintenance activities including lawn service during testing days.
- Adjusted classroom temperatures to comfortable levels.
- Made no announcements from the school's public address system.
- Made sure that lunch and breakfast schedules were on time.
- Temporarily halted school bells that announced schedule changes.
- Thanked students and teachers, at the end of each testing session, for their focus and reminded them of our goal of making an "A" grade.
- Provided complimentary breakfast and snacks to teachers each testing day and organized a celebration lunch at the end of the testing period.

At the beginning of our turnaround year, the students offered me a challenge. They decided that since I expected an "A" rated performance from them, they wanted something in return when they delivered. The challenge was for me to publicly kiss a pig after running three laps around the play field. I hurriedly bought a porcelain pig that I used as a reminder and motivation each morning on the public address system. I thought I could get away with kissing the beautiful porcelain pig. Little did I know that the teachers and students made arrangements with a neighboring farm to have a gargantuan pig brought to the school for me to kiss. Well, not only did I run my laps and kiss the pig but I had to do this in front of the entire school community and mass media. This activity was extremely unifying and motivating; a great way to culminate months of hard work.

With the extensive focus on curriculum, instruction and assessment and helping the students reduce test anxiety, we believed we had done everything possible to prepare students for the big test. The question at this time was, "What is the evidence that the school would achieve its desired "A" rating?"

YOUR ACTION PLAN AND CHECKLIST

Identify test taking skills and strategies to be taught

Design lesson plan component to teach, practice and record test taking skills and strategies

Survey students about test concerns they have

Establish a forum to help alleviate fears about the test

Inform parents of test expectations for seamless communication between home and school

Notify cafeteria staff of nutritional expectations and any changes in lunch schedules during testing

Notify maintenance department and vendors of test dates so there will be no interruptions or disruptions during testing

Establish school-wide expectations for testing

Set a goal that challenges and motivates students to win

ANSWER THE QUESTION: ARE WE THERE YET?

Up to this point I have shared steps and procedures we took at the school center to set the stage for our dramatic turn-around. Teachers articulated students' academic and behavior progress in evidence-based terms. The discussions in the teachers' lounge took a more problem solving and supportive tone. Team collaboration meetings were truly focused on student progress toward proficiency. Teachers' records also indicated a plan of instruction, enhancement, remediation and re-teaching for each student. At any given time a teacher was able to provide up-to-date evidence of student progress.

Check individual student progress

The weekly graphing of student benchmark progress contributed significantly to students' motivation to learn and succeed. They had tangible evidence of their progress each week and they knew if the 85% or better goal was not achieved, all was not lost. Through re-teaching and re-testing, the undesirable score could be reversed. Students also knew that success was publicly rewarded and celebrated. I believe the decrease in off task behaviors was a result of the laser-like academic focus that was happening throughout the school. It was amazing to see that students were beginning to articulate their learning targets and what they needed to do in order to improve their performance.

Evaluate stakeholders' feedback

It seemed like every adult on the campus smiled more and had extra perkiness in their stride. We all began to own every child. The body languages said, "I am pleased to be part of this success story."

Parents were becoming more engaged in school activities. This was evidenced by the increased numbers at parent teacher conferences and participation in other school events. Additionally, there were more phone calls with inquiries about student academic and behavior progress. Volunteerism in classrooms and at school events had improved tremendously. From an administrative perspective, the school community was operating with one accord.

The community partners provided snacks for Saturday tutorials, sponsored our honor roll assemblies and were guest speakers for classrooms and school-wide assemblies. We received discounts on lunches for teacher appreciation and students' celebrations. Our business partners helped to provide items for student incentives. Our cultural diversity celebrations grew bigger with more community involvement. There was definitely a change in the school.

I was feeling very confident that all planning, processes and procedures were in place and we were doing a great job of comparing our own data to ourselves. Since I wanted no surprises from the 'big' test, it was now time to compare ourselves to the state standards and to other district and state schools with similar demographics. So we examined and compared current performance data to the data from the same time the previous year. All grade level benchmarks results showed an improvement, but to our distinct pleasure, our third grade scores were among the highest in the district with similar schools.

We immediately jumped into action and had the third grade teachers lead staff discussions on what they were doing. We hired substitute teachers or used administrators to supervise classes while teachers spent time in third grade classes to learn what was making the difference. Other schools were calling to find out what we were doing. The entire school got a huge boost in confidence as we headed toward the final days before the administration of the state test.

Identify remaining challenges

While there was some very positive data it was also evident that there was still work left to be done. Far too many students were not proficient readers. Students in the Exceptional Student Education and the English Language Learners programs were still showing some academic weaknesses. The writing scores of the fourth grade students, while improving, had opportunities for improvement.

Stay on track with a checklist

The climate was favorable to face the brutal facts. In the team collaboration meetings the hard questions were asked.

- Which teachers were getting the greatest results? Why?
- Which reading and mathematics skills were showing the greatest challenges? Why?
- Were students doing better with the narrative or expository writing prompts? Why?

❧ Are the right students being targeted for additional support? How do you know?

❧ Are the same students consistently scoring below the 85%? Why?

❧ Which benchmark skills need to be reviewed consistently each week? Why?

❧ Are there enough materials and equipment to meet the teaching and learning needs? If not, what materials and equipment are needed?

❧ Are the daily teacher lesson plans targeted to all ability levels in the classroom? How do we know?

❧ Is there enough rigor in the weekly assessments? How do we know?

❧ Are the daily instructional practices aligned with the state standards and benchmarks? How do you know?

❧ Are students still excited and motivated? How do you know?

The questions came fast and furious; so did the responses to correct the problem areas. Within grade levels; teachers looked at each other's data and reached out for help. Strategies for teaching and re-teaching were constantly shared.

Ask and answer the hard questions

Strategies to correct weaknesses across subjects and grades were immediately addressed. For example, comprehension reading skills needed improvements across all grades so additional professional development took place and every teacher emphasized reading comprehension skills in all subject areas. The data showed that students were doing better in narrative writing so real world experiences were brought in the writing classes to improve expository writing skills. Many 'how to' projects were done and students wrote about them. Sample student writings from the state were analyzed and students constantly revised their own writings using the writing rubric. Hands on activities in mathematics and science were expanded; so was co-teaching opportunities between mathematics, writing, and computer lab teachers and regular classroom teachers. Samples of students' work were analyzed at each team meeting. The discussion around the student work was extremely helpful to both teaching and learning. The Item Specifications were once again reviewed to ensure that everyone was on a unified course of action.

Principal Cover assists students with a classroom assignment

Florida Department of Education Website September 5, 2003

Intensify monitoring and support

The data also identified specific student needs and individualized plans were developed. As a result, more students were added to the list of those who were getting tutorial support. Data chats and goal setting sessions were scheduled on a regular basis with individual students. Student-run parent conferences were established. At the meetings, students used personal portfolios to share their performance with their parents and showed their plan of action for success on the test. Administration increased walk-through visits to classrooms and had more frequent individual meetings with teachers and students. The use of technology was intensified to improve individual performance in specific skills.

There were constant checks to gauge student endurance and motivation levels. The student incentives helped to keep their motivation levels high and the success on the weekly graphs brought personal gratification. Teacher resilience was also important, so administration organized and executed special teacher celebrations which will be detailed in the seventh chapter. So to answer the question, "Are we there yet?" If we measured attitudes, perceptions, preparations, efficacy and camaraderie we were unquestionably there. However, some lagging indicators remained so we pressed on. We vigorously and passionately continued to teach, monitored performance and made adjustments as needed.

As we got closer to the first day of test administration, we noticed heightened interest from the media, the school district's central office as well as other schools. Eyes were on our experiment. We were visited regularly and constantly got

News

Pucker up: Educator kisses pig after grades improve

Delray Times, October 15, 2003

questions from other schools. This was particularly exciting because before the turnaround process began, we were the one calling other schools to get help. This made me think about the book, The Little Engine that Could, which was read by all classes on my first day as principal of "X" Elementary School.

On the first day of testing, and throughout the testing period, the students displayed a level of confidence that was uplifting. They had positive remarks about their performance and promised that we would achieve our goal. They told me to get ready to kiss the pig. Indeed, they lived up to their promise. We made the first "A" grade in the school's history and the first "A" rated school among the neighboring elementary schools. We outperformed many schools in our category. And yes, I ran my three laps around the playfield and I kissed the huge drooling pig in front of the entire school.

The School Accountability Report sums up the results of the drastic changes that took place across grades three, four and five.

School Year	% Level 3 or Higher in Reading	% Level 3 or Higher in Math	% Meeting The Writing Standard	% Making Learning Gains in Reading	% Making Learning Gains in Math	% Lowest 25% Making Learning Gains in Reading	School Grade	Percent Tested
2002-03	47	56	91	67	88	61	A	100
2001-02	34	28	73	57	72	62	C	98

This chart shows a significant increase in Reading, Math and Writing scores within a two year period including 2003 when the school made its first "A". Significant also is that 100 percent of students were tested in 2003. Note: prior to 2002 proficiency was weighed differently, hence the reason for sharing two years' results.

Chapter V :: Answer the Question: Are We There Yet?

YOUR ACTION PLAN AND CHECKLIST

- [ ] Intensify monitoring and support

- [ ] Vigilantly review student data

- [ ] Make any necessary adjustments to maximize learning

- [ ] Examine and compare the data for evidence of progress

- [ ] Ask and answer the difficult questions

- [ ] Solicit feedback from stakeholder groups

- [ ] Monitor the endurance level of staff and students

- [ ] Build test momentum with confidence and team spirit

- [ ] Share the excitement with others

LEAD WITH A PURPOSE

Create a vision

Leadership, for me, is using a variety of skill sets to work efficiently with people in order to accomplish a vision. My vision for "X" Elementary School was to help all students see that they had great potential and they had to believe that they could thrive in school, be lifelong learners and consequently help to improve their school's rating.

It was also my vision to help teachers recognize that they had the capacity to effect positive academic and behavioral changes in their students. To accomplish this task I had to effectively lead, promote and manage a school culture that was favorable to successful teaching and learning.

Be courageous

I started the journey with a determination to significantly improve student achievement and through the process to transform attitudes, behaviors, perceptions and actions. Along the way, I realized that an underlying mission was to prove that children from poor and disadvantaged families can and will succeed when:

➤ They are provided the essential tools
➤ The teachers around them use the necessary pedagogical skills and strategies

➢Teachers demonstrate the will to do the required work and are of the fervent belief that the children in their charge deserve a high quality education.

Continuously learn

Through it all, I was able to improve my own leadership skills and reaffirm that my actions and behaviors were critical to the success of our school. As the principal, I was the instructional leader, the operations manager and the model for truthfulness, sincerity, and justice. The turnaround process that I led required me to use all these leadership skills and more.

As the instructional leader, my ongoing task was to promote and maintain a positive learning environment. I accomplished this in many different ways. I worked alongside our teachers and became a learner with them. In that regard, I attended all professional development sessions and completed the necessary follow-up classroom activities. I occasionally became a substitute teacher to allow time for teachers to learn from each other or I sometimes taught a class in order to give the teacher a few moments of down time. I continuously and publicly thanked the staff for their commitment to our students and our school. On occasions, I personally served them lunch and snacks. Teachers generally appreciate the gift of time so on non-student school days or at other appropriate times I would allow them to leave work a little earlier than usual.

Delray Times, October 15, 2003

Reward achievements

I learned the names of all the students so I was able to personalize my conversations with them. Student accomplishments were celebrated in a variety of ways.

- Each marking period we had a full breakfast honor roll assembly.
- We invited parents and the community and always had student performances and a motivating guest speaker.
- We established criteria for Student of the Month and each month the winner had lunch with the principal, seated at a special table in the school's cafeteria or at a local restaurant, sponsored by community partners.
- I provided opportunities for students to talk with me when they had concerns. With permission from their teacher, they could visit me and freely express their issues.

Communicate effectively

A positive learning environment is one in which expectations are communicated in clear and concise terms. Not only did we have a working school improvement plan that had input from the entire school community, but we also met weekly as a faculty to share vital information and resolve concerns. We developed schedules that gave our collaborative teams opportunities for professional growth and development. As the principal, I established an open door policy that provided teachers easy access for communicating with me. We were frequently visited by various news media outlets, so I learned how to communicate with and utilize the media to publicize the good things that were happening in our school.

Embrace diversity

Acknowledging and celebrating cultures create a sense of belonging. Our school had a significant number of families from several different cultures. Not only did I ensure that the school library had books and other materials representative of diverse cultures, but we had events where we brought awareness and celebrated cultural diversity. The Cultural Awareness Day was a major event. Every class participated. They shared history, customs, traditions, values and beliefs of groups and peoples and we always tasted foods. I made sure that all school committees and leadership teams had diverse representations.

Be accountable

In my role as instructional leader, I was accountable for a viable instructional program that met the needs of every student. It was therefore my responsibility to assign teachers to the most appropriate teaching positions commensurate with their skills and experiences. Research based instructional strategies were employed, monitored and assessed on an ongoing basis. Academic goals, based on state standards and benchmarks, were developed, skills were taught using a variety of approaches to meet the needs of a diverse student body, and students were given opportunities to reinforce skills. Lesson plans had to reflect instructional strategies for all ability levels.

It was my expectation that all students received feedback on assignments in a timely manner. Identified students received additional academic help through organized and structured tutoring. Along with school staff, we systematically reviewed school data and I made necessary adjustments.

Be resourceful

Through the allocation of school funds and resources, I ensured that students and staff had adequate materials and supplies to meet their various teaching and learning needs. I applied for grants and appealed to our community for additional resources. I used Title 1 funds to hire additional teaching and support staff to help meet the needs of the very diverse student population.

Be proactive

In addition to my participation in team meetings, I conducted daily classroom visits and provided feedback to teachers in a timely manner. I looked for certain elements or got engaged in some specific activities when I visited classrooms:
- Checked for the posted objectives and skills.
- Observed interactions between teacher and students and among students.
- Reviewed samples of students' work posted in the classroom.
- Conducted random reviews of students' portfolios.
- Reviewed the alignment of lesson plans and instructional practices.

- Talked to students about what they were learning.
- Reviewed the weekly graphs that showed students' performance.
- Checked for cleanliness and order in the classroom.

We kept parents abreast of the curriculum expectations and provided help on how they could assist at home. Students who did not have much support with homework at home, could complete homework at school with teacher supervision. The school-age child care program became an extension of the school, in that academic skills were reinforced in this after school program.

The teachers in the after-school childcare program communicated regularly with the classroom teachers. The communication was centered on reinforcing grade level skills in reading, writing and mathematics with all students in the program but importantly, targeted students got help with their identified deficiencies. The strategies employed during the after school program were different from those used during the regular school day. This gave students other ways to learn the skills.

Positive school environments are usually well managed and are reflections of places where students and staff feel safe. At our school we established a school-wide behavior plan. The expectations of the plan were taught, practiced and monitored, and the plan itself was revisited often. Behavior contracts were developed for targeted students, and as needed, we organized wrap around services (see table below). Two guidance counselors provided the approved in-class guidance curriculum that included character development. They, along with the Behavior Health Professional, worked with several community agencies

WRAP AROUND SERVICE AGENCIES

Therapeutic Services	Case Management or Medical
South County Mental Health	Children's Home Society
Youth Services Bureau	Community Action Program
Chrysalis Center	St. Mary's Child Development Center
Aid to Victims of Domestic Violence	Wellness Center
Center for Group Counseling	Health Care District-Healthy Kids
Children's Case Management	Medicaid
Center for Family Services	Palm Tran
Parenting Education Center	
Multilingual Psychotherapy Center	
Community Intervention Research Center	
Mental Health Center – Listen to Children	

to provide a variety of services to the children and their families. We held parent-teacher conferences regularly and parents were undoubtedly partners in the discipline process.

The student and family handbook outlined school and school district rules, regulations, and policies. Some of these included health requirements for attendance, testing and other important dates for the school year, the school-wide discipline plan and the use and policies related to technology, textbooks and the library. Included also were contact information for pertinent school staff, information regarding volunteering at school and tips on how to support school activities. The handbooks were written in different languages. Parents were expected to sign, indicating receipt of the handbook and they were encouraged to occasionally review its contents throughout the school year.

Teachers and staff also had a handbook which outlined contractual obligations, guidelines for the effective delivery and monitoring of curriculum, instruction and assessment, expectations for working with colleagues, and how to hold successful parent teacher conferences.

Included also were expectations for attendance and participation at school based or school district required meetings. Also in the handbook, readers would find a description of the processes and procedures that relate to the collection and deposit of monies being collected for school activities. When issues arose, I dealt with them quickly and fairly. Like the parents, teachers and staff had to sign for the receipt of the handbook.

Epitomize integrity

Leaders have a moral and ethical responsibility to respect the rights and dignity of others. This turnaround year speedily brought many people together to make a difference in the school. It was therefore, important to build cohesive teams, understand the needs and idiosyncrasies of each person when decisions were being made and when actions were taken. Importantly, it was of the essence to value the opinions of others as we took this remarkable journey together. The staff handbook included a section that outlined clear expectations of how to treat others with respect and dignity.

Build trust

During the turnaround process we were in a changing environment so building trust was critical to developing and accomplishing our shared vision. Change is sometimes difficult and will therefore meet resistance. However, in our situation,

CHARACTERISTICS OF EFFECTIVE LEADERSHIP

Visionary	Accountable
Courageous	Resourceful
Lifelong learner	Proactive versus reactive
Rewards performance	Epitomizes integrity
Good communicator	Builds trust
Embraces cultural diversity	

the stage was set early in the process. With the various meetings held we were deliberate about engaging stakeholders. In many different ways the vision was communicated and the positive tone for high expectations was set. This attitude permeated throughout the school. I remained steadfast to the mission and all my actions, behaviors and language demonstrated this. The school district, our parents and the community, the school staff and importantly our students, had placed confidence in my abilities to lead our school to a successful turnaround.

In the end the victory was shared. It was for students who now had references of what personal and school success looked and felt like. It was for the staff that was relentless in their efforts to successfully complete the vision. It was for a community that could now boast their first "A" rated school. It was for parents who wept with joy when their children beamed with pride. It was for the school district that could show off a school that had beaten the odds.

This process reaffirmed that while leaders must possess the necessary tangible leadership skills and deportment they must also lead with heart and soul. Through this transformation process many personal and professional lives were changed.

YOUR ACTION PLAN AND CHECKLIST

Set the tone for a conducive, safe, and supportive school environment

Lead with confidence, courage and humanity

Prioritize the monitoring of teaching and learning

Reward performance fairly and ethically

Make any necessary adjustments to achieve the goal

Lead and manage by example

Learn alongside staff

Hold on-going meetings to communicate progress

Embrace, promote and foster diversity

Monitor use of resources

Keep abreast of student and teacher needs

Monitor the testing environment

Identify needs and plan relevant professional development

Identify and utilize wrap-around services for students as needed

Develop and monitor the use of the student and family and staff handbooks

CELEBRATE TO STIMULATE

Motivate using accountablity

Achievements were celebrated throughout the turnaround year. It did not matter how small or large the accomplishment, we found ways to reward performance. We operated from the premise that when celebrations are linked to achievement, increased motivation occurs. I still remember times of walking in the hallways or being engaged in general conversations with students and a popular question they would ask was, "Did you see that I improved on my graph this week"? For those students who did not have positive scores on their tests their usual comment was, "I did not score 85% this week, but I promise I will next week because I am going to work harder".

To the students, success came with accountability. I clearly remembered the day when Student L made his first 85% on a reading test. His joy brought him to tears and his classmates celebrated and cried with him. That was the beginning of many more scores of 85% or greater for this student. Teachers were also motivated by their students' achievements. Each week teachers compared their class averages to see whose class had the top scores. Their mission for the following week was to outperform the competition. Teachers took this seriously as they motivated students to attain their best personal and collective performances.

Acknowledge individual and group achievements

The celebration activities took many different formats. We celebrated with individual students, with classes within grades, and entire grade levels. For example:
- When a student earned a score of six on a practice writing prompt, I read the essay at a grade level assembly.
- Students who completed more questions on their weekly test than they did the previous week had their efforts acknowledged.
- A student was rewarded when significant improvement was made on a weekly test. I visited the classroom and gave prizes such as books, special pens or pencils, book bags, school supplies, and sometimes even an ice cream from the cafeteria.
- The students always receive a sticker on their graphing spreadsheet when the 85% or greater goal was met.

Individual classes or entire grades were honored for outstanding academic and behavior achievements. For example, if all the students in a fourth grade class scored above a three on the practice writing assignment there was reason for celebration. Similarly, when no student scored a one on the practice writing it was also acknowledged.

Rewards included pizza parties, and extra time in the playground with another top scoring class at the same grade level. Whole class ice cream socials were very popular rewards, and so were moments spent with the principal. Teachers also generated their own rewards. Each class had its own celebrations or they connected with adjoining classes in celebration. They wrote and performed exciting chants centered on the test. They developed mantras that served as personal or group motivation.

There was a huge celebration when 100% of the students scored at least 85%; when there were no disciplinary infractions that week and when the percentage of students scoring at least 85% was greater than that of the class next door. We also celebrated birthday parties, but the focus had to be on academic skills or themes like Measurement, Patterns, and Fractions or 'Did you know?' where students researched the origins of identified party foods and shared their findings during the party.

Make rewards tangible

At the beginning of the school year, students in grades three through five were given a survey. They were asked two questions. The first was, "If you had three wishes, what would they be?" They listed the wishes in order of preference. Secondly, "If you got ten dollars, how would you spend it?" They also had to explain the reason for their choices. The responses were filed by classes. Every third through fifth grade student completed the survey. When new students registered in school, we made sure they completed the survey.

Naturally, there were wide variations in the survey responses. These included buying a house or car for mom, owning a first bicycle and getting a doll or a remote controlled car. Some students wanted to help pay the rent while others just wanted to go to the neighborhood McDonalds for a Happy Meal. At the end of each week after the results of the weekly tests were posted, students who scored at least 85% got their names placed in a bowl.

There was a bowl for each of the three grade levels. One name was pulled from each bowl during the morning announcements so the entire student body witnessed. When the names were drawn, I would go to my file folder to see what the students' surveys showed. By the end of the day, wishes would be granted. Sometimes parents had to come to school to pick up the prize if it was too big for the student to take on the school bus or too heavy for the walk home. We were able to make these wishes a reality with donations from our community partners, from funds we raised by hosting school events and through donations from faculty and staff.

Delray Times, October 15, 2003

Accentuate academic achievements

The Principal's Honor Roll assemblies provided another opportunity to celebrate success. Each marking period we had an honor roll breakfast that was catered by the cafeteria. These assemblies were made very special. A full breakfast was served, the tables were covered with linen, there was always a guest speaker and students performed. All students from kindergarten through the fifth grades who were getting an award went to the assembly in the cafeteria. All other students watched the event on the television in their classroom. The music teachers always had students perform. Parents and community representatives were invited. Parents looked forward to this event and students worked hard so they would be at the Principal's Honor Roll breakfast.

Highlight performance and support employees

To show appreciation for our instructional and support staff teams, and to maintain high motivation we celebrated with our staff. On occasions, the professional development activities were held in a conference room at one of the local top rated hotels. Administration treated the staff to catered lunches and on non-student attendance days such as teacher planning we had luncheon meetings at local restaurants.

Through ongoing raffles, teachers received items like gift cards and classroom supplies compliments of our community partners. Sometimes they got to leave work earlier than they normally would. We had potluck or catered parties at co-workers' homes. There were times on Friday afternoons when we just stayed at school and talked, with no specific agendas.

It was not unusual for the school administration to periodically teach classes simply to give teachers a break. We highlighted classroom accomplishments at faculty meetings. When I conducted classroom visits, I always left a note sharing at least one positive thing I observed. I frequently provided updates on school-wide academic and behavior achievements. There were times when I asked school district personnel, from the assessment department, to present updates on our school's data. Without fail, we looked at how other schools were progressing; not just the schools with similar demographics but

WAYS TO CELEBRATE SUCCESS

Promote healthy competition
Acknowledge individual and group achievements
Make rewards tangible
Accentuate academic achievements
Highlight performance and support employees
Make celebrations as instantaneous as possible

schools that consistently scored "A" grades. We became extremely competitive.

There were some events that would not be categorized as celebrations but they brought the school community together in a fun and stress-free manner. For example, the staff participated in the student talent shows. We chuckled about these performances for weeks afterward. When our students performed in the community, we were there to cheer them on. We had school carnivals that involved families and the entire school community.

In the external evaluation conducted at the end of the year, it was not possible to quantify the impact that these celebrations had on the overall success of the school, but it was obvious that they greatly impacted attitudes and perceptions which in turn created a very positive and much improved school environment.

The reform model showed that celebrating achievements contribute to overall school improvement. This model taught us many other lessons that will be discussed in more details in the next chapter.

YOUR ACTION PLAN AND CHECKLIST

Establish a system to acknowledge and celebrate achievements

Organize various types and formats for rewarding achievements

Determine criteria and format for celebrations

Reward students and staff

Survey students on their wishes for incentives

Make rewards tangible and immediate

Acknowledge individual and group achievements

Identify resources to support celebratory activities

Publicize achievements

Include parents and community partners in celebrations

LESSONS LEARNED

The goal of this school turnaround model was to significantly improve student achievement at an urban elementary school, and through the course of action improve the school's letter grade. Through the process we learned a lot about ourselves and the resilience and determination of children. We learned that most people will make and support change when they see a reason to do so. We developed and honed personal and professional skills and strategies that not only changed the trajectory of our school but became a model for others. We learned that success is contagious.

Competent and ethical leadership is critical in a school's transformation process

This process reiterated that competent and ethical leadership is essential to a successful school transformation. All along the journey I had to review and refine my communication and collaboration skills. I had to be fair and honest both in words and deeds. I had to be an astute student. I modeled and promoted acceptable behaviors and I, unquestionably, had to lead with both heart and soul.

Begin with the end in mind

The goal was to become an "A" rated elementary school, the first in the community, so every action taken was directly related to realizing this goal. All school activities were aligned to the goals and objectives of the school improvement plan. My favorite question when presented with ideas teachers wanted to implement was, "How is this activity aligned with our established goals and objectives?

We constantly referred to the plan in order to ensure that we were staying true to the mission. However, while we were determined to achieving this goal, we were resolute in teaching skills and strategies that would help our students become lifelong learners. We did not prepare them just for success on the high stakes state test.

Data should drive the plan

The school's academic and discipline trend data showed that over time many students were not making the state required adequate yearly progress. The data also showed that some teachers were making significant gains with their students while others were not achieving similar successes.

To add to this scenario, the discipline data showed an abundance of disciplinary referrals that demonstrated inconsistencies in how disciplinary issues were being handled. In round table discussions with the adults on the campus there were differences of opinions on conditions in the school. It was not surprising when blame was being thrown in many directions. Using the data we were able to arrive at a common understanding of the real situation that maintained the support for the reform model.

Develop realistic and measurable goals and objectives

Based on state and school district standards and expectations, we developed reasonable goals and objectives. We learned that in order to significantly improve academic performance, a unified and systematic approach had to be taken; one that included the entire school community working together in a supportive and collaborative atmosphere. We ensured that all goals and objectives were measurable and aligned to the mission.

Know the curriculum targets

One of the first steps we took was to develop a working knowledge of what children should know and be able to do. We organized what skills should be taught before and after the test and in which order. We relied on information in the Item Specifications for the State Standards. A variety of resources including technology and textbooks were used to teach the skills. We ensured that academic skills were reinforced with activities like field trips and other real world experiences.

Know all students' abilities and performance levels

All teachers should have current information about students' performance. This information will be beneficial when designing individualized action plans and communicating with parents. Additionally, students should know their performance levels in relationship to proficiency. The results of the school's weekly tests as well as the school district's required diagnostic and common assessments provided information about students' current performance levels compared to proficiency. This knowledge helped both teachers and students to stay focused, engaged and motivated.

Teachers should know their content

Teachers must be experts in the subjects they teach. Likewise, they should have a wealth of instructional strategies to teach and engage all types of learners. Along the same lines, teachers must differentiate instruction in order to meet the needs of all students in their classrooms.

In order to improve the content knowledge of teachers, we participated in ongoing professional development sessions which included follow-up activities. I monitored instruction daily for evidence of the incorporation of the new strategies learned in the professional development activities.

Teach test taking skills and strategies

While the teaching of content for mastery is essential, students should also be taught test taking skills and strategies. We included the explicit teaching of test taking skills and strategies in daily classroom instruction. This approach created a strong sense of test awareness but also minimized testing anxieties.

Teach, re-teach and provide timely feedback

All teachers should teach new skills directly and implicitly, followed by multiple opportunities for individual and guided practice. Re-teaching and providing immediate feedback were expected. When we observed classrooms we looked for evidence of direct teaching, and re-teaching strategies, as well as strategies providing and eliciting feedback. Time was built into classroom schedules for re-teaching, feedback and retesting.

Use a variety of assessments

Student data should come from a variety of reliable sources. Assessments should be done as often as possible and the results used to inform instruction. In addition to our school based weekly tests, we administered school district common assessments. In both cases, results were provided in a timely manner making it possible to make the necessary instructional adjustments.

Teach students the format and conditions of the standardized test

Students should be taught the format and expectations for before and during test administration. Familiarity with proctors and the rooms contribute to students' level of comfort on test days. While this created extra work for school staff, the benefits to students are immeasurable. This strategy helped to alleviate some test anxieties. We followed directions that were similar to those used in the administration of the standardized test.

Technology is a valuable tool for enhancing, practicing and remediating academic skills.

For technology to be effective, there should be an alignment with software and skills being taught in the classroom and staff must be trained accordingly. In our school, the computer teacher attended grade level meetings in order to create the alignment. Both classroom and lab computers were utilized.

We also learned that some students need additional time and opportunities for repetition to enhance learning. Hence, additional learning opportunities for students were established. Organized tutorial sessions using research based materials and taught by qualified teachers should be employed. We established before, during, and after school and sometimes Saturday tutorial sessions for targeted students. I believe these sessions contributed significantly to students' learning gains.

Take time to celebrate success

Celebrating achievement helps to motivate both students and teachers. Throughout the turnaround year, we used every possible opportunity to acknowledge and celebrate the efforts of both students and staff. We celebrated large and small achievements and while we were not able to quantify the impact to academic improvements, the activities contributed to improved morale, solidarity and pride.

Prioritize collegial collaboration

Time should be built into the schedule for teachers to plan and work together. We thoroughly benefited from the time spent learning from each other, discussing student achievements and strategizing on how to make our school a better place in which to teach and learn. On the external evaluation, teachers commented that the time they had to plan and work together was very constructive both on a personal as well as professional level.

We reaffirmed that parents and guardians are valuable partners in the teaching and learning process. Every opportunity should be given to get parents and guardians involved in their child's education. We dramatically increased involvement and engagement through regularly scheduled parents' meetings, home visits, parent representation on some school committees, and through the use of the agenda books. Additionally, school administrators made positive phone calls home on a regular basis.

Establish a safe and orderly school environment

Students and staff should feel safe at school. We addressed safety with a school-wide discipline plan that employed a unified, fair and consistent approach. The plan was taught, practiced, and revised as necessary. Discipline issues were dealt with immediately.

Align all resources to the goals and objectives of the reform model

All resources should be allocated to support the activities in the plan. We conducted no extraneous spending. Neither was time spent on activities that were unrelated to the mission's goals and objectives.

Standardized test scores do not tell the complete story

Our main goal was to become an "A" rated school and in this we were successful. However, the test scores did not show the gradual improvements in beliefs, attitudes, perceptions and actions, the daily sacrifices made by school staff, or the students' smiles and confidence that surfaced. The test results certainly did not reflect the positive changes across the school.

School is not over when the state test has been completed

After the administration of the state standardized test, there tends to be an attitude that school is over so it is time to relax and wait for test results. At our school that was not the case. We jumped in full gear continuing to teach and assess curriculum standards and benchmarks. We also did some temporary and periodic restructuring. For example, fourth grade teachers worked with the third grade students and teachers on writing. We had roundtable discussions about persistent instructional weaknesses and revised our strategies. We gave credit for the areas of strengths. While collaboration and planning sessions still focused on the instruction of academic skills for the current year, time was used for reflecting on what worked as evidenced in the test results, and strategies in the reform model were revised consequently.

LESSONS LEARNED

Competent and ethical leadership is critical in a school's transformation process

Begin with the end in mind

Data should drive the plan

Develop realistic and measurable goals and objectives

Know the curriculum targets

Know all students' abilities and performance levels

Teachers should know their content

Teach test taking skills and strategies

Teach, re-teach and provide timely feedback

Use a variety of assessments

Teach students the format and conditions of the standardized test

Technology is a valuable tool for enhancing, practicing and remediating academic skills

Some students need additional time and opportunities for repetition to enhance learning

Take time to celebrate success

Prioritize collegial collaboration

Parents and guardians are valuable partners in the teaching and learning process

Establish a safe and orderly school environment

Align all resources to the goals and objectives of the reform model

Standardized test scores do not tell the complete story

School is not over when the state test has been completed

CONCLUSION

'I am beside myself'

Sun-Sentinel, June 2003

I have had the most wonderful career serving in instructional and administrative positions at a variety of school centers and at the school district level. Teaching graduate level students who are pursuing degrees in education has also expanded my knowledge of the research about what works in education. Each experience presented unique rewards and challenges that helped me cultivate my skills and widen my perspectives. My goal has always been that wherever I serve, I leave an indelible mark, making a positive difference in the lives of children and the adults who encircle them.

I served as principal of "X" Elementary School, in the southeast region of the United States for four years; four of the most memorable years of my career. Of my many leadership positions, this school presented some of the greatest opportunities for development amongst all stakeholders including myself. The year I started, the school's data showed a dismal picture of students' academic achievements toward local, state and federal requirements. An equally bleak situation was evident in students' behaviors. The school had a revolving door for teachers and administrators. Similarly, parents and community engagement in school activities was less than desirable. This deteriorating situation gave rise to the development and implementation of the Reform Model which is at the heart of this book.

The school's Reform Model provided evidence that dramatic student achievement is possible when schools employ a well-defined and systematic approach. This includes using multiple data sources to identify and remedy the problems, creating a sense of urgency to tackle the issues, setting purposeful, measurable and achievable goals, improving instructional practices through targeted and specific professional development, utilizing a variety of research based instructional strategies, and monitoring accomplishments through ongoing assessments.

The model also showed that it is important for schools to establish a culture where high achievement is the standard; that everyone must be held accountable and achievements must be highlighted. Clearly, this model proved that children in poverty are capable and will succeed when the school environment is organized, supportive and conducive to their learning needs and learning styles.

Many of our graduates carried the 'can do' attitude to their respective middle and high schools. Over the years, I have interacted with several who have graduated from college or who are still pursuing college degrees in areas that include education, medicine, engineering and technology. Teachers who have now transferred to other schools have shared that they are constantly asked to provide or model best practices because they have the reputation and experience of a successful school turnaround.

In 2003 when the school was triumphant in achieving its first "A" rating, the news media was there to celebrate with us. One of the newspaper headlines quoted me saying "I am beside myself…" and here I am again using those words but not for the same reasons.

For several years after its victorious first "A", the school continued the implementation with minor adjustments to the reform strategies. There were some administrative changes but, for the most part, the instructional staff remained stable and the same level of funding and support continued. During this time the school rating fluctuated between A and B ratings. However, over the past few years, the school has experienced drastic reductions in funding and other resources. There have been several administrative and instructional changes. Strategies from the reform model are almost nonexistent. So, as you can imagine, I am beside myself because once again the school is experiencing a state of decline, resulting in it being classified as a critically low school.

The conditions that created the significant improvement in student achievement at "X" Elementary School have been eroded largely due to the removal of funding, targeted support and other resources. It is my hope that education policy developers and other decision makers, lobbyists, as well as advocates for urban education will read this school's story and commit to working for the allocation of adequate funding and appropriate resources to urban schools. "X" Elementary School proved that through the implementation of a strategic and unified process, low performing schools can be transformed, but sustaining the high achievement requires dedication and targeted resources.

Whether your school is big or small, serves few or many students needing academic and or behavioral interventions, and is located in an urban, suburban or rural area, this book proves that all children can and will succeed.

Believe that you are in the right place and this is the right time to create a sense of urgency around the needs of your students and your school. Use your courage, your influence, your will, along with these proven, practical strategies and processes to provide the best possible learning environment for your deserving students.

What I know for sure is that, armed with this book, schools facing performance challenges can be significantly transformed into scoring an "A" rating in record time.

BIBLIOGRAPHY

Bennett, Carol. (2013). *What is balanced literature?* Retrieved from http://www.wresa.org/ERR/Module %201.

Collins, Jim. 2001. *Good to great: Why some companies make the leap and others don't.* HarperCollins Publisher.

etools4Education. (2013). *Effective teacher.* Retrieved from http://www.online-distance-learning-education.com/effective-teacher.html

Fogarty, Robin. 1999. *How to raise test scores.* SkyLight Training and Publishing, Inc.

Horton, Henry W. Kodak. *Thirteen traits of effective leaders.* Retrieved from http://www.au.af.mil/au/awc/awcgate/au-24/horton

Payne, Ruby K. 2005. *A framework for understanding poverty. aha! Process,* Incorporated.

Stanbury, Meris. (2011, September 9). *Five characteristics of an effective 21st-century educator.* Retrieved from http://www.eschoolnews.com/2011/09/09/five-characteristics-of-an-effective-21st-century-educator

Strauss, Valerie. (2013, May 2). *Why collaboration is vital to creating effective schools.* Retrieved from www.washingtonpost.com/blogs/answer-sheet/wp/2013/05/02/why-collaboration-is-vital-to-creating-effective-schools

Swenson, Paula. (2013). *Characteristics of effective teaching.* Retrieved from http://www.ehow.com/about_5061110_characteristics-effective-teaching.html

The Holden Leadership Center. (2009). *Leadership characteristics.* Retrieved from http://leadership.uoregon.edu/resources/exercises_tips/skills/leadership_characteristics eratur

The Hunt, (2013, June 30). *11 facts about education and Poverty in America.* Retrieved from http://www.dosomething.org/tipsandtools/11-facts-about-education-and-poverty-america#

RECOMMENDED READING

Airasian, Peter W. (2005). *Classroom Assessments: Concepts and applications* (5th ed.). MA: McGraw Hill.

Barbour, Chandler, Barbour, Nita, and Scully, Patricia. (2011) *Families, Schools, and Communities: Building partnerships for Educating Children.* NJ: Pearson.

Bulent, Atalay. (2006). *Math and the Mona Lisa: The Art and Science of Leonardo da Vinci.* New York: Collins.

Casey, Samuel C. (2000). *No excuses: Lessons from 21 High-performing, High-poverty Schools.* Washington DC: The Heritage Foundation.

Covey, Stephen. (2006). *The Speed of Trust: The One Thing that Changes Everything.* New York: Free Press.

Doyle, Denis P. and Thomas, David A. (2009) *Leading for Equity: The Pursuit of Excellence in Montgomery County Public Schools.* MA: Harvard Education Press.

Editor, Weber, Karl. (2010). *Waiting for Superman: How we can Save America's Failing Public Schools.* New York: Public Affairs.

Gallagher, Kelly. (2009). *Readicide: How schools are killing reading and what you can do about it.* Ma: Stenhouse Publishers.

Gladwell, Malcolm. (2005). *Blink: The power of thinking without thinking.* New York: Back Bay Books.

Hunt, John. (2009). *The art of the idea and how it can change your life.* New York: powerHouse Books.

Jackson, Yvette. (2011). *The pedagogy of confidence: Inspiring high intellectual performance in urban schools.* New York: teachers College Press.

Kafele, Baruth K. (2009). *Motivating black males to achieve in school and in life*. VA: ASCD.

Lencioni, Patrick. (2002). *The five dysfunctions of a team: A leadership fable*. CA: Jossey-Bass.

Medina, John. (2008). *Brain rules: 12 principles for surviving and thriving at work, home, and school*. WA: Pear Press.

Piper, Watty. (1976). *The little engine that could*. New York: Platt & Munk.

Thomas-El, Salome. (2003). *I choose to stay: a black teacher refuses to desert the inner city*. New York: Kensington Publishing Corp.

NEWSPAPER & OTHER HEADLINES

The Right Grade: Educator Janice Cover is largely responsible for increased FCAT scores. Delray Times, October 15, 2003

Students losing FCAT Fear: They are more prepared for the test that begins today. Sun-Sentinel, South Florida, February 21, 2001

Pucker Up: Educator Kisses Pig After Grade Improves. Delray Times, October 15, 2003

A School That Just Tries Hard. Sun-Sentinel, August 17, 2003

Principal Helps Students Bloom. Sun-Sentinel, August 17, 2003

School Takes No Excuses. Florida Department of Education Website September 5, 2003

School Moves Past Disadvantage. Palm Beach Post, May 11, 2003

School plans programs for summer camp: Principal plans to keep students' minds sharp. Sun-Sentinel, January 2002

Program at School rewards Good Conduct: School Yields Results. Sun-Sentinel, January 2002

Turn-Around Principal: High Stakes Leadership. Principal magazine, September/October 2004

"I am beside myself..." Principal Janice Cover is ecstatic as she learns about her school rating. To go from a low C to an A! Sun-Sentinel, June 2003

ACKNOWLEDGEMENTS

Much thanks to:

My parents Gwendolyn and Alexander Scott, who taught me the importance of a good education, a sense of community and how to dream big.

My many colleagues and friends all over the world, who rode the many waves with me and carried me on their shoulders.

Pam, your help and support will never be forgotten.

All my former students who pushed me beyond limits.

Patrick, Patrice, Julian, Marlon and Patsy for always believing I could.

Improving Schools
Consulting Services
Proven ♦ Practical ♦ Pace-setting

WE ARE COMMITTED TO WORKING AS YOUR PARTNER TO SIGNIFICANTLY IMPROVE AND SUSTAIN HIGH STUDENT ACHIEVEMENT.

In its total school transformation model, Improving Schools Consulting Services will send a team of professionals to partner with the school professionals to develop, implement and monitor curriculum, instruction and assessment as well as other related school systems to significantly improve student achievement. We believe in the total engagement of the student, the school and the home in this school transformation approach.

Improving Schools will work with the school to:
- Conduct a school needs assessment
- Develop a School Improvement Plan as identified in the needs assessment
- Implement the school improvement plan of action
- Develop an effective monitoring system using a variety of assessment tools and resources
- Establish an ongoing systematic reporting system that informs the school community
- Create a system to celebrate student and school success

WORKSHOPS • SPEAKING
TEACHER PROFESSIONAL DEVELOPMENT

www.improvingschoolsinfo.com

consulting@drjanicecoverbooks.com
1.561.313.4772

EDUCATIONAL SERVICES DELIVERED THROUGHOUT THE UNITED STATES AND INTERNATIONALLY

www.ingramcontent.com/pod-product-compliance
Lightning Source LLC
Chambersburg PA
CBHW071222160426
43196CB00012B/2382